THE COOKBOOK
FOR THE CANNABIS LOVER!

Blunts & Baking

INCLUDES OVER 20 RECIPES OF CANNABIS INFUSED DESSERTS, BREADS, SAUCES, AND MORE!

RECIPES BY
ANDI "AUNTIE BEE" BOYKINS

Blunts & Baking

by

ANDI "AUNTIE BEE" BOYKINS

www.jsnacks.com

COPYRIGHT © 2024 BY ANDI J. BOYKINS

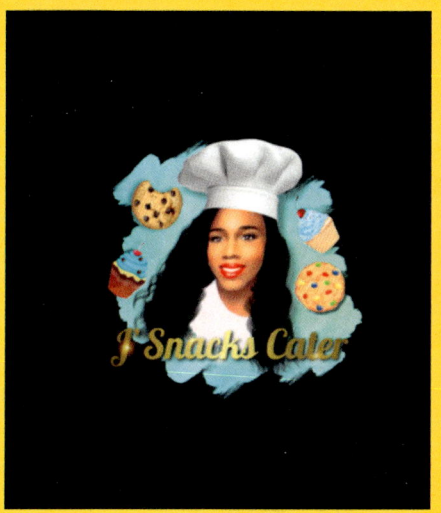

ALL QUOTES, RECIPES, PHOTOS, AND OWNED BY J'SNACKS CATERING, LLC

PRINTED IN THE UNITED STATES OF AMERICA

FIRST PRINT EDITION 2024
ISBN: 9798322524144

FRONT COVER IMAGE & BOOK DESIGN BY
ANDI J. BOYKINS

PUBLISHED BY: J'SNACKS CATERING, **LLC**

WASHINGTON, D.C.

WWW.JSNACKS.COM

INTRO

The consumption of cannabis-infused food, often referred to as edibles, carries significant importance in both culinary and therapeutic contexts.

Cannabis-infused food offers a unique avenue for culinary creativity, providing chefs and home cooks with an opportunity to explore new flavors and textures. From savory dishes like cannabis-infused pasta sauces to sweet treats such as infused chocolates and baked goods, the versatility of cannabis as an ingredient adds depth and complexity to culinary creations.

Beyond its culinary appeal, cannabis-infused food holds promise as a therapeutic delivery method for cannabis-derived compounds, particularly cannabinoids like THC and CBD. When ingested, cannabinoids are metabolized by the liver, resulting in a slower onset of effects compared to inhalation but with longer-lasting duration. This sustained release mechanism is advantageous for individuals seeking prolonged symptom relief, such as those managing chronic pain or insomnia.

Moreover, the culinary experience of consuming cannabis-infused food can enhance the overall therapeutic effect through sensory enjoyment and relaxation. The ritualistic aspect of preparing and sharing infused meals can foster social connection and promote well-being, aligning with holistic approaches to health and healing.

In conclusion, cannabis-infused food represents a convergence of culinary innovation and therapeutic potential. From its ability to elevate gastronomic experiences to its role in providing sustained symptom relief, the importance of incorporating cannabis into edible products is evident. By embracing responsible consumption practices and fostering culinary creativity, cannabis-infused food has the potential to enrich both the dining experience and the realm of holistic wellness.

DOSAGE

There are several considerations and best practices to keep in mind when consuming cannabis-infused food. First and foremost is dosage awareness. It's crucial for individuals to start with a low dose, especially if they are new to consuming infused food, and gradually increase their dosage over time as they become familiar with their tolerance levels. Additionally, consumers should carefully read recipes to determine the potency of the meal .

Each recipe is paired with one of Auntie's Infused Cannabis Butters. There a 3 flavors. The Purple Haze, Seafood, and the Garlic Herb Butter. Each butter is infused with over 10,000mg of THC, slow-cooked for hours, and color-whipped into an 8oz Jar. Each recipe includes a dosage range of 2 tablespoons - 1/3 cup of the infused butter that accompanies that particular recipe. This dosage range is recommended for moderate tolerance levels. Those with higher tolerance levels will most-likely use as much as they can handle. Also, remember each recipe can be made WITHOUT the cannabis infused butters for those who don't want that HIGH KICK to their food. All butters can be purchased ONLY AT www.jsnacks.com .

AUNTIE'S INFUSED BUTTERS

SEAFOOD

GARLIC HERB

PURPLE HAZE

WWW.JSNACKS.COM

**WE DO
NOT
COUNT
CALORIES
OVER
HEA**

AUNTIE'S INFUSED JERK "ME CHICKEN SANDWIVHES

SERVINGS: 4   PREPPING TIME: 15 MIN   COOKING TIME: 45 MIN

INGREDIENTS

4 Boneless Chicken Thighs

1/3 cup of store bought butter

Between 2 Full tablespoons and a 1/3 cup of

(INFUSED GARLIC BUTTER)

4 BRIOCHE BUNS

Favorite JERKSAUCE & Favorite HONEY

(MEASURE TO YOUR LIKING)

Salt

Pepper

Onion Powder

Garlic Powder

Mayo

Arugula

Red Onion

2 cups shredded cheese

1/4 cornstarch

small can of condensed milk.

Grab your INFUSED BUTTERS at www.jsnacks.com

DIRECTIONS

1. Clean & season chicken with Salt, Pepper, Onion and Garlic Powder inside a mixing bowl.
2. Add at least 1/2 cup of jerk-sauce to chicken and toss around in bowl making sure everything is covered. Let chicken marinate in fridge for at least 3 hours.
3. After marinating, add store bought butter and add at least 2 tablespoons of Infused Garlic Butter to a heated saucepan or skillet. As butter is melting, add marinated chicken thighs with all the juices to skillet and cook chicken on each side for about 5 minutes or until inside of chicken is 165 degrees.
4. Remove chicken to a cutting board and rough chop chicken. (Will be Hot) Toast your Brioche Buns once you chop chicken. Spread Infused Garlic Butter on Toasted Buns and put everything to the side and start cheese sauce.
5. To a bowl add 2 cups of shredded cheese and toss in about 1/4 cup of cornstarch. Make sure all the cheese is covered in cornstarch. To a saucepan/pot and a small can of condensed milk over medium heat. Once it begins to simmer start adding the cheese slowly, continuously stirring. It will form and thicken up. You want a creamy consistency so keep heat low. Add pepper/salt to taste.
6. Once cheese sauce is made to your liking, lets take a couple of tablespoons of jerk-sauce and a couple tablespoons of honey to a bowl and mix and then heat in microwave for 40 seconds.
7. NOW it's time to assemble your jerks (LOL). Add mayo to your top and bottom of toasted buns. Place chicken on bottom bun. Top chicken with Jerk-Honey mix followed by cheese-sauce.
8. To the top bun add arugula and red onions. Now it's time to close sandwich up, bringing the top bun over to the bottom bun and closing everything together.
9. Add a side of pickles, chips, or fries to complete. AND ENJOY!!!

NOTES

Store leftover chicken and cheese in air tight containers in fridge for up to 3 days. Chips, pickles, or fries go great as a side. Butter the brioche buns and toast them for more of an authentic taste. Cook chicken throughly. Remember the INFUSED GARLIC BUTTER is what kicks these sandwiches up. You can use regular butter instead, but if you want the KICK, between 2 tablespoons and 1/3 cup of my INFUSED GARLIC BUTTER is recommended. Its up to you how much you want to incorporate.

Grab your INFUSED BUTTERS at www.jsnacks.com

WE ALL HAVE ROLLS BABY!

Auntie's Infused Strawberry Cheesecake Cups

🍴 9 cakecups   🕐 60 minutes

Jumbo Cupcake Tray (9 cups)

INGREDIENTS

For the cookie cups:
150 g (store brought) unsalted butter
Between 2 Full tablespoons and a 1/3 cup
of (INFUSED PURPLE HAZE BUTTER)
100 g Sugar
150 g Light brown sugar
1 egg room temperature
1 tsp Vanilla extract
250 g Self Rising flour
1 tsp Salt

For the filling and decoration:
150 g Soften Cream Cheese
100 g Powder Sugar
1/3 cup Heavy Cream
1 tsp Vanilla extract
1 container of Strawberry Glaze
10 Strawberries
1 box graham cracker crumbs

NOTES
Store your strawberry cheesecake cookie cups in an airtight
container, in the fridge for 2-3 days or freeze for up to 1 month.

DIRECTIONS

Start by making the cookie cups:

1. Preheat the oven to 350°F Lightly grease a JUMBO cupcake tray with a little butter.
2. In a large bowl, beat all the butter and two sugars together until creamy.
3. Mix in the egg and vanilla extract.
4. Fold in the flour and salt to form a cookie dough.
5. Take 2-3 heaped tablespoons of cookie dough and roll it into a ball. Place in one of the cupcake holes. Repeat until all the cookie dough has been used up. Making 9 cookies cups in total. (about 2-3 tablespoons of dough per cup).
6. Bake for 12-14 minutes until golden and firm around the edge, but the middle is still pale and soft.
7. Remove from the oven and immediately use the base of a small jar, pot or teaspoon to press down the middle of each cookie to shape them into cups. Pop in the fridge for 30 minutes or until the cookie cups have cooled completely.

Make the cheesecake filling

1. Rinse and slice 10 strawberries. Mix them in a bowl with the container of strawberry glaze and set aside.
2. Place the cream cheese into a bowl and then sift in the powder sugar. Gently mix until just combined.
3. Add the heavy cream and vanilla extract and whisk together until the cheesecake mixture is thick, smooth and holds its shape.
4. Fill the base of each cookie cup with the cheesecake filling and top with the strawvberry glaze mixture. Then finish by sprinkling graham cracker crumbs on top. ENJOY!

LET THAT STOMACH HANG BOO

Auntie's Crab Boil

SERVINGS: 6   PREPPING TIME: 20 MIN   COOKING TIME: 45 MIN

Ingredients

FOR THE CAJUN SEAFOOD BOIL:

- 3 quarts water
- 1 (12-ounce) can of beer
- 3 tablespoons Cajun seasoning
- 1 tablespoon Old Bay seasoning
- Hot sauce, to taste
- 1 medium yellow onion, roughly sliced into half-moons
- 1 large lemon, cut into wedges for serving
- 12 ounces andouille sausage, sliced into rounds
- 1 lb baby potatoes, red or gold (or a mix of both)
- 1 lb pre-cooked snow crab leg clusters, fresh or frozen
- 1 – 1 ½ lbs jumbo shrimp, deveined, shell-on or peeled
- 4-6 ears sweet corn on the cob, I use the mini ones
- 4-6 hard boiled eggs

FOR THE GARLIC BUTTER SAUCE:

- 1/2 cup (1 stick) store bought butter
- 1/3 cup of INFUSED SEAFOOD BUTTER
- 10 cloves minced garlic
- 2 tablespoons lemon juice
- 1 tablespoon Old Bay seasoning
- 1 tablespoon fresh chopped parsley
- 1 teaspoon Cajun seasoning
- 1 teaspoon smoked paprika
- Sliced sautéed onions

Directions

- Prepare the boil. In an extra large stockpot or dutch oven (about 10 quarts or larger) over medium-high heat, combine the water and beer (if using). Bring the liquid to a boil. Then season the boil with the Cajun seasoning, Old Bay seasoning, and a few dashes of hot sauce- to taste. Stir all the ingredients well to thoroughly combine. Let the mixture boil for 15 minutes.

- Add the andouille & potatoes. Carefully add the andouille sausage rounds and baby potatoes into the pot, stirring well to fully combine with the boil. Let the andouille and potatoes cook for 15-20 minutes- or until the potatoes are just about fork-tender.

- Add the seafood & corn. Gently nestle the snow crab clusters into the pot along with the shrimp and corn on the cob. Be sure that everything is fully submerged under the boil and carefully stir to ensure all ingredients are well combined. Continue boiling for another 5-7 minutes, cooking until the shrimp is pink. Meanwhile, prepare the garlic butter sauce.

- Make the garlic butter sauce. On a separate burner, in a small saucepan over medium heat, combine the butters, garlic, lemon juice, Old Bay seasoning, parsley, Cajun seasoning, smoked paprika, and sliced onions. Stir all ingredients and simmer until the onions are sautéed and the sauce is well combined, stirring often, about 5-7 minutes. Then remove from heat.

- Assemble cajun seafood boil with sauce. Line an extra large baking sheet with foil/parchment paper (or newspaper if you'd like!). Use a spider strainer to remove the seafood boil contents from the pot and place onto the prepared baking sheet along with the hard boiled eggs Note: If you'd like your garlic butter sauce to be thinner, you can add some of the seafood boil broth to adjust to desired consistency. Now, this is the fun part! Pour the garlic butter sauce over the seafood boil ingredients. Then use your hands (fitted with disposable gloves if desired) to toss the sauce with everything, smothering every nook and cranny in sauce.

- Serve seafood boil. Feel free to serve Auntie's Seafood Boil as-is with everyone just grabbing what they'd like from the baking sheet directly (it's the chaos and messiness of seafood boils that are so fun!) or divide the boil onto individual plates to serve if you prefer. Serve immediately with lemon wedges, if desired. Be sure to sop up any runaway garlic butter sauce. Enjoy!

ROLL
DAT
SHIT
UP!

Prep Time : 15 min   Cook Time : 15 min   Servings : 6-9

INGREDIENTS

- 2 cup all purpose flour-a little extra for rolling
- 1 tablespoon baking powder
- 1/4 teaspoon baking soda
- 1/2 teaspoon salt
- 1/4 cup granulated sugar
- 6 Tablespoons very cold cut butter (store brought butter)
- 3/4 cup cold buttermilk
- 3/4 cup frozen blueberries
- 3 tablespoons of Infused Purple Haze Butter

Lemon Glaze
1 Cup powdered sugar
2-3 Teaspoons of lemon zest
1-2 Tablespoons fresh lemon juice

INSTRUCTIONS

- Preheat oven to 450
- Cube 6 tablespoons of store bought butter in small squares , place in a small bowl and place in the freezer for 10 minutes
- Melt 3 tablespoons of Infused Purple Haze butter put to the side.
- Grease the pan you are using generously, I use a cast iron skillet
- In a large mixing bowl sift together the flour, baking powder, baking soda, salt and granulated sugar
- Once the store bought butter is cold enough using a fork or pastry cutter cut the butter into the flour mixture until the butter looks like small pebbles or peas
- Remove the buttermilk from the fridge and slowly mix it into the flour mixture.
- Fold in blueberries carefully, if using frozen they won't break as easily
- Turn the mixture onto a floured surface and with floured hands press the dough into a 1/2 inch thick rectangle.
- Do Not Roll or the berries will break
- Use a biscuit cutter or glass and cut the biscuits and place them in the pan.
- You will need to reform the dough to cut more biscuits, you should be able to get 5-6 depending on the size
- Brush the biscuits with the melted infused butter generously.
- Bake in preheated oven for 10-14 or until golden brown
- While the biscuits are baking mix the glaze ingredients to the consistency you like using fresh lemon juice.
- Once the biscuits are done let them cool for 5 minutes
- Drizzle glaze on biscuits

IT'S SMELLING LOUD IN HERE

Auntie's Grilled Cheese w/ Fried Green Tomatoes.

SERVINGS: 2   PREPPING TIME: 10 MIN   COOKING TIME: 20 MIN

INGREDIENTS

1-2 green tomatoes (cut up into 1/4 inch thick slices)

1 egg

1/3 cup of milk

1 cup crushed Corn Flakes

1/4 cup vegetable oil

Between 2 Full tablespoons and a 1/3 cup of

(INFUSED PURPLE or GARLIC BUTTER)

4 slices of sourdough bread

2 slices pepper jack cheese

2 slices cheddar cheese

4 slices thick cut bacon

favorite ranch dressing

DIRECTIONS

- In a medium bowl, beat the egg and add milk. In another bowl, add cornflakes and crush finely. Dip slices of green tomatoes into the egg, and then into the cornflakes, shaking to remove any excess. Do this for all the green tomato slices.

- Add vegetable oil into a large skillet, heating it over medium heat. Add the green tomato slices, cooking on each side until golden brown, about 3 minutes per side. Remove the tomato slices and place on paper towels to remove any extra oil.

- Using another paper towel, wipe clean the skillet to remove vegetable oil. Heat the skillet again on medium heat.

- Spread Infused Butter onto each side of each slice of bread. Place 2 slices of bread, butter side down, onto the skillet. Stack 2 slices of pepper-jack cheese, add 2 slices of bacon, and the 2 slices of cheddar cheese. Top with remaining buttered slice of bread.

- Cook until the bottom of the sandwich is brown, to your liking, and then carefully flip and brown the other side. Do this to the other sandwich. Serve alongside fried green tomatoes and some ranch dressing. Enjoy!

Notes
The best type of bread for this recipe is thicker varieties, like sourdough or whole wheat. You can even use English muffins instead if you'd like! I love this sandwich with pepper jack cheese because it's a little bit of spice with the tomatoes on the side, but you can use any type of cheese you'd like – American, Provolone, Muenster and more!

YO, MILEY WATS GOOD!

Strawberry Shortcake Bars

12 Bars 50 min.

9X9 baking pan

INGREDIENTS

VANILLA BARS:

1 box vanilla cake mix

2 large eggs

⅓ cup vegetable oil

Between 2 Full tablespoons and a 1/3 cup of (INFUSED PURPLE HAZE BUTTER)

STRAWBERRY CRUMBLE:

1 3oz. package strawberry gelatin mix, dry

1 3 oz. package vanilla instant pudding mix, dry

½ cup (1 stick) store brought unsalted butter, softened

1 cup all-purpose flour,

COOL WHIP FROSTING:

1 8 oz. package cream cheese, softened

1 cup powdered sugar

1 teaspoon vanilla extract

1 8 oz. tub Cool Whip topping, thawed

DIRECTIONS

- Mix the cake mix, eggs, and vegetable oil together until well combined. Add between 2 Full tablespoons and a 1/3 cup of (INFUSED PURPLE HAZE BUTTER).

- Press. The dough into the bottom of a 9x9 baking pan lined with parchment paper and greased. Bake for 20 minutes.

- Bake. The crumble by mixing together the strawberry jello mix and vanilla pudding mix with the flour and butter and bake for 5 minutes.

- Whip. Together the cream cheese, powdered sugar, vanilla extract, and cool whip until light and fluffy.

- Spread. Once the bars are cooled from the oven, spread the cream cheese and cool whip frosting evenly on the bars.

- Sprinkle. The baked crumble on top of the cool whip frosting. Cut into 12 squares and enjoy!

NOTES:
- Store the assembled bars in the refrigerator for up to 1 week.
- Crumble. When the crumble comes out of the oven, throw it in a container and place it in the freezer for 10 minutes to help quickly cool. You don't want this crumble going on the frosting hot.
- Store. Store leftover Strawberry Shortcake bars in an airtight container in the refrigerator for up to 1 week.
- Freeze. You can freeze these tasty bars once they are made and cooled. For easy access cut them into squares and freeze them in an air-tight container or a freezer gallon bag. When ready to eat, eat as a frozen treat, or thaw in the refrigerator and enjoy!

WHERE MY DAMN LIGHTER AT?

Marry Me Chicken

Prep Time : 5 min
Cook Time : 25 min
Servings : 4

Ingredients :

- 650 g Chicken breast (skinless and boneless), About x4
- 50 g Plain flour
- Between 2 Full tablespoons and a 1/3 cup of (INFUSED GARLIC or PURPLE HAZE BUTTER)
- 3 Garlic cloves, Peeled and crushed
- 150 g Sun dried tomatoes, Drained
- 1 tsp Dried oregano
- 2 tsp Paprika
- 150 ml Hevay Cream cream
- 200 ml Chicken stock
- 50 g Parmesan cheese, Grated
- 15 g Fresh basil leaves
- 1/2 Lemon, Just the juice
- All your favorite chicken seasonings

Directions

1. Coat the chicken breasts in the flour.

2. In a large, deep frying pan, heat desired amount of infused butter over a medium heat. When it's melting, carefully add the chicken breasts. Cook for 5 minutes. Flip and cook for a further 5 minutes.

3. Remove the chicken breasts to a plate, turn the heat under the pan to low and desired amount of infused butter, add the garlic, sun-dried tomatoes, oregano and paprika. Stir for 3-5 minutes until the garlic is softened.

4. Add the heavy cream, stock, parmesan and plenty of salt and pepper and give everything a good stir.

5. Sit the chicken back in the sauce. Put the lid on the pan and cook for 5 minutes. Turn the chicken and cook for another 5 minutes.

6. Check the chicken, make sure it is cooked through. Remove the pan from the heat, sprinkle over the basil leaves and the squeeze of half a lemon.

7. Plate on top of mash potatoes, rice, or pasta. You can also pair with veggies.

Notes :

- Cooking time: This will vary slightly depending on the thickness of chicken breasts. If in doubt, check with your meat thermometer.
- Lemon juice: When you add the lemon juice at the end, the sauce can curdle a little if it's very hot. If if does, just remove the chicken breasts to serve and give the sauce a good whisk.

IT'S FRIDAY AND IMMA GET YOU HIGH TODAY!

Eat My GLIZZY

Prep Time : 10 min
Cook Time : 15 min
Servings : 6

Ingredients:

1 Green and Red Peppers

1 Red Onion

Ketchup

Mustard

6 Beef Hot Dogs

6 Hot Dog Buns

Relish

Between 2 Full tablespoons and a 1/3 cup of (INFUSED GARLIC or PURPLE HAZE BUTTER)

Notes :

Enjoyed best when shared.

Directions:

- Dice onion and slice both green and red peppers.

- To a skillet add 1/3 cup infused butter. As it melts add peppers and onions.

- Cook until sautéed or soft in texture. Remove from heat set aside.

- For the hot dogs: Preheat a grill pan or outdoor grill to medium-high heat.

- Cook the hot dogs until they're hot throughout, 4 to 5 minutes. Remove from the heat and set aside for plating.

- Turn off the heat on the grill pan or outdoor grill. Use the residual heat from the pan or grill to warm the hot dog buns, about 5 minutes.

- Place the hot dogs in the buns and assemble according to your liking. Starting with relish, then condiments, and topped with peppers and onions. Enjoy!

Notes :
Enjoyed best when shared.

DON'T OVERDOSE ON CANNABUTTER

LEMON BUTTER POUND CAKE

Prep Time : 20 min
Cook Time : 1hr 50min
Servings : 8-10

Ingredients:

1 1/2 cups all-purpose flour

1 teaspoon baking powder

1/2 teaspoon salt

1 cup (2 sticks) store brought butter, softened at room temperature

1 cup sugar, plus 1/3 cup

4 eggs

2 teaspoons pure vanilla extract

1/4 cup lemon juice, plus 1/3 cup

Between 2 Full tablespoons and a 1/3 cup of (PURPLE HAZE BUTTER)

LEMON BUTTER POUND CAKE

Directions

- Preheat the oven to 350 degrees F. Butter a 6-cup loaf pan and line it with parchment or waxed paper. In a medium bowl, combine the flour, baking powder, and salt.

- In a stand mixer (or using a hand mixer), cream all the butters. Add 1 cup of the sugar and mix. With the mixer running at low speed, add the eggs one at a time. Add the vanilla.

- Working in alternating batches, and mixing after each addition, add the dry ingredients and 1/4 cup of the lemon juice to the butter mixture. Mix until just smooth.

- Pour into the prepared pan and bake until raised in the center and a tester inserted into the center comes out dry and almost clean (a few crumbs are OK), 65 to 75 minutes.

- Meanwhile, make the glaze: In a small bowl, stir together the remaining 1/3 cup sugar and the remaining 1/3 cup lemon juice until the sugar is dissolved.

- When the cake is done, let cool in the pan 15 minutes (it will still be warm). Run a knife around the sides of the pan. Set a wire rack on a sheet pan with sides (to catch the glaze) and turn the cake out onto the rack. Peel off the waxed paper.

- Using a spoon or pastry brush, spread glaze all over the top and sides of the cake and let soak in. Repeat until the entire glaze is used up, including any glaze that has dripped through onto the sheet pan. Let cool at room temperature or, wrapped in plastic wrap, in the refrigerator (Well wrapped, the cake will last up to a week). Serve at room temperature, cut in thin slices.

WE AIN'T NEVA LOSING WEIGHT BABY

Lick Me All Over
Infused D'usse Sweet Potato Pie

8 servings · 2 hrs

INGREDIENTS

4 medium (342 g) sweet potatoes, baked

1/2 cup (113 g) store bought butter

1 cup (198 g) granulated sugar

2 teaspoons (9 g) vanilla extract

2 large (100 g) eggs, beaten

1/2 cup (114 g) milk, whole or evaporated

1 (9-inch) unbaked pie crust

Between 2 Full tablespoons and a 1/3 cup of

(PURPLE HAZE BUTTER)

1/2 cup of D'usse Liqour

NOTES

DIRECTIONS

- Preheat the oven to 400° F. Scrub the sweet potatoes until clean, prick them 4 to 5 times with a fork. Place onto a baking sheet and bake for 45 – 50 minutes until the sweet potatoes are tender when pricked with a toothpick.

- Remove from the oven and allow to cool until they can easily be handled. Peel the skin from the sweet potatoes and place the sweet potatoes into a large mixing bowl. Reduce the oven heat to 350° F.

- Add all butters to the sweet potatoes and mash until smooth. Add the sugar(s) to the sweet potatoes and mix until well combined. Add the vanilla extract, milk, and the eggs. Add the D'usse. Mix until well combined. Pour into the unbaked pie crust.

- Bake the Pie. Bake the pie until the center of the pie is set, about 1 hour. Remove the pie from the oven and allow to cool slightly.

- Serve the pie warm or allow to cool before slicing.

NOTES

You can also use 3/4 cup brown sugar in this pie recipe for a Brown Sugar Sweet Potato Pie version. You can use either light or dark brown sugar, based on your preference. Marshmallow is optional and is added on top of pies RIGHT BEFORE PIE GOES IN OVEN

NOPE! NOT UN-BIGGING MY BACK

Sugar N My Tank Cookies

🍴 15 servings   🕐 30min

Ingredients:

1 ½ cups all purpose flour, add 2 extra tablespoons for thicker cookies

1 ½ teaspoons baking powder

¼ teaspoon salt

½ cup store bought butter, softened slightly but still cool

1 cup granulated sugar

1 large egg

2 ½ teaspoons pure vanilla extract

1/3 cup lemon juice

3 cups of powder sugar

2 Full tablespoons of (PURPLE HAZE BUTTER)

¾ cup sprinkles, see note

Instructions:

- Preheat oven to 350°F. Line two baking sheets with parchment paper.

- In a bowl whisk together 3 cups powder sugar, 1 teaspoon of vanilla and a 1/3 cup lemon juice until consistency is thick like icing. Set to the side.

- In a bowl, whisk together flour, baking powder and salt. Set aside.

- Using a hand mixer or stand mixer, beat all butters until smooth. Slowly pour in the sugar, mixing as you pour. Beat sugar and butter for a minute, until light and fluffy. Add egg and vanilla extract, mixing until combined and scraping the sides of the bowl as needed. Add in flour mixture and mix until just combined. Add 1/4 cup sprinkles (see note) and stir by hand until combined.

- Scoop 2-tablespoon portions of dough and roll into a ball. Place ¼ cup sprinkles on a plate and press the tops of the dough balls in sprinkles. Place dough balls onto prepared baking sheet leaving about a couple inches for spreading. I like to mound the dough balls higher rather than wider so that they bake up on the thicker side.

- Bake for 9-11 minutes. The edges should be completely set, and the centers should look slightly under cooked. See note about shaping the cookies immediately after baking. Place the baking sheets on wire racks to cool. Repeat with remaining dough once the baking sheets are completely cool.

- Once cookies are cooled, spread powder sugar icing on them and top with the last 1/4 of sprinkles.

Notes:

Butter should be softened slightly. It should not be starting to melt, or losing its shape.

Immediately after the cookies come out of the oven place a round glass, bowl, or cookie cutter (larger than the cookie) upside down over the top of the cookie. Gently but quickly swirl the glass/bowl/cookie cutter in a circular motion. The edges of the cookie will bump against the inside of the glass creating a perfectly round shape. Note: This only works when the cookies are hot, straight from the oven, and still on the baking sheet.

SLOB
ON MY
CHICKEN
COBB

2 servings   35 minutes

Ingredients

1 Butterhead of Lettuce
4 slices of Bacon
2 siced Boiled Eggs
Salt & Pepper
1 sliced Cucumber
1 sliced whole Tomato
Shredded Cheddar
1 Pack of All-Purpose **"EUPHORIA"** seasoning
1 1/2 cups Flour
2 tablespoons olive oil
Vegetable oil for cooking
2 whisked eggs
2 medium skinless boneless chicken breasts
Favorite Dressing

Directions

- Chop and add lettuce into a large bowl, and season with some salt & black pepper. Massage the leaves well for 3 minutes. Let stand for 10 minutes. (Optional but does help the lettuce soften and soak up some flavors).

- Wash and dry the chicken. Pound it just a little bit to ensure even cooking. Add to a plate and toss in olive oil. Then season chicken breast with "Euphoria" seasoning packet. Set to side.

- Prepare 2 bowls. One for flour and one for whisked eggs.

- One by one, dip each chicken breast first in flour, beaten egg, and then back in flour.

- Warm up cooking oil in a large nonstick skillet over medium-high heat. Cook chicken for 4 minutes on both sides or until golden brown and crispy. . To ensure chicken doneness, use a kitchen thermometer to register 165 degrees Fahrenheit inserted into the thickest part of the chicken.

- Set aside on a plate with a paper towel to absorb the excess oil. Slice chicken into smaller strips or just cubes in bite-size pieces.

- Plate lettuce and arrange all the vegetables on top. Add egg, bacon, and cheese. Add crispy chicken strips to the center and drizzle with your favorite dressing. Season with salt and black pepper if needed. Serve while the chicken is still warm.

Pussy Pink Poundcake

Poundcake:

Serves : 6-8
Cooking Time Varies

1 Box of Strawberry Cake Mix
(Eggs/Milk/Water/oil according to instructions)

Between 2 Full tablespoons and a 1/3 cup of
(PURPLE HAZE BUTTER)

icing:

3 cups powder sugar

2 teaspoons cake batter artificial flavoring

2 tablespoons of water or milk

How to Make:

Preheat oven too 350 degrees F.

Butter a 6-cup loaf pan and line it with parchment or waxed paper.

Mix cake mix and box ingredients together. Add **infused butter** to mix and combine well

Pour mix into loaf and bake according to box instructions. Check center with a fork or tooth pick to make sure its completely done. Let cook for 15-20 minutes once finished.

Combine powder sugar, milk/water, and cake batter flavoring and mix it until thick consistency. It's okay to add more powder sugar or water/milk until desired thickness.

Once cake is cooled, drizzle icing ALL OVER POUNDCAKE, and serve!

AUNTIE'S INFUSED BUTTERS

SEAFOOD

GARLIC HERB

PURPLE HAZE

WWW.JSNACKS.COM

**WE DO
NOT
COUNT
CALORIES
OVER
HEA**

MEATBALL GRINDER

INGRIDIENTS

3 cups bread cut into small cubes
1 cup milk
1 lb ground beef
3 eggs
3 cloves garlic
3/4 cups Parmigiano Reggiano cheese grated
2 tbsp fresh flat leaf parsley finely chopped
1/2 tsp kosher salt
1/2 tsp freshly ground pepper
4-5 cups basic tomato sauce or your favorite tomato sauce
Italian Seasoning
Oregano
Between 2 Full tablespoons
and a 1/3 cup of (INFUSED PURPLE HAZE or GARLIC BUTTER)
1 footlong sub or bread of choice
2-4 slices fresh mozzarella cheese
Parmigiano Reggiano cheese grated for serving
Banana Peppers
Red Onions

PREP TIME: 20 MINUTES MINS
COOK TIME: 1 HOUR HR
SERVES: 1

DIRECTIONS

- Heat the oven to 400°F. In a large skillet or saucepan with a lid, heat up your tomato sauce over medium low heat. Add in infused butter, and all listed seasonings. Stir and let slow cook.

- Place the bread cubes in a bowl and cover with milk, tossing so that all the cubes are saturated. After 1-2 minutes the bread should be soggy and wet. Using your hands, squeeze out as much milk as possible. Use your fingertips to break up the bread into very small breadcrumbs.

- In a large bowl, mix together the bread, ground beef, eggs, garlic, parmesan, flat leaf parsley, salt, Italian seasoning, oregano, and freshly ground pepper. You want to mix everything so that it's homogenous, but loose – don't work the meatball mixture too much.

- By this time your sauce should be simmering with several bubbles breaking the surface. Form large meatballs (I make and 6-7 big ones) and drop them directly into the sauce. Simmer in the sauce, partially covered, over medium heat, flipping occasionally. Simmer gently until cooked through, about 25-30 minutes.

- Cut the sub roll in half so you'll have two sandwiches, then cut lengthwise. Top both sides of the bread with a generous amount of sauce and a bit of grated parmesan. Place the meatballs on the bottom half and top with slices of mozzarella and some more parmesan.

- Top with onions, banana peppers, and a pinch of seasonings and place in oven.

- Bake until the cheese is gooey and melted. Enjoy!

Auntie's Shrimp & Grits

Prep Time : 10min　　　**Cook Time : 20min**　　　**Servings : 4**

INGREDIENTS

1 lb peeled & deveined shrimp small size; 51-60 ct

4 cups chicken broth

1/2 cup heavy cream

1 cup quick grits* not instant

2 tbsp store bought butter

1/3 cup of **INFUSED SEAFOOD BUTTER**

1 1/2 cups medium cheddar cheese grated

1/4 cup parmesan cheese grated

salt & pepper to taste

old bay seasoning to taste

parsley fresh, for garnish

DIRECTIONS

- Bring chicken broth to rolling boil in large pot. Whisk in grits, salt and pepper and reduce heat to medium and cook 10-15 minutes, stirring occasionally.

- Once grits are completely cooked, add heavy cream, store bought butter and cheeses. Stir to combine. Taste and adjust seasonings.

- Preheat a large skillet over medium heat. Add desired amount of infused seafood butter. Once melted add shrimp, salt, pepper and old-bay to taste. Cook for 3 minutes on each side or until shrimp are bright pink and thoroughly cooked. Remove from heat.

- Spoon grits into bowl and top with shrimp mixture. Garnish with parsley, if desired. Serve immediately.

Notes:
 I suggest following the package of grit directions for the cooking time. I do not recommend using instant grits as those are precooked and then dried. Lemon slices and garlic toast are great additions to this meal.

WE DO NOT COUNT CALORIES OVER HEA

Auntie's Infused Canna-Butter

INGREDIENTS

Slow Cooker
8 oz to a 1lb store bought butter,
½ oz to a 1 oz decarboxylated cannabis
Wooden spoon
Cheesecloth and/or mesh strainer
Mason Jars or Air Tight Container

DIRECTIONS

Preheat oven to 200 degree F.

To decarboxylate cannabis, Break up cannabis and spread out on a sheet pan lined with parchment paper.

Bake cannabis for 20 minutes, rotating every 5 minutes. The aroma will start to seep out from the oven.

Once cannabis is decarboxylated, grind finely and set to the side.

Turn on slow cooker to medium heat setting and add store bought butter. Once melted then add the finely ground decarboxylated cannabis. Mix well with a wooden spoon and cover with lid.

Simmer gently for at least 4 hours or up to 24 hours. The longer it cooks the stronger it will be. Stirring every half hour to make sure the butter isn't burning. If you have a kitchen thermometer, check to make sure the temperature doesn't reach above 180°F.

After at least 4 hours, strain with cheesecloth or mesh strainer into a container. Let the butter cool to room temperature. Use immediately, or store in an airtight container (a well-sealed mason jar will work) in the refrigerator or freezer for up to six months.

BANANA PUDDING BROWNIES

YIELD: 12   PREP TIME: 5 MIN   COOK TIME: 20 MIN

Ingredients:

1 box Brownie mix
2 eggs
Between 2 tbsp-1/3cup of INFUSED PURPLE HAZE BUTTER
3 tbsp vegetable oil
5 tbsp water
6 ounces cream cheese, softened
⅓ cup milk
1 small box instant banana pudding mix
Box of Vanilla Wafers

Directions:

- Preheat the oven to 350*.
- Grease or spray an 8x8 baking pan.

- Using a large mixing bowl, add the brownie mix, 1 egg, INFUSED PURPLE HAZE BUTTER, vegetable oil and the water (or the ingredients listed on your box) make according to the box directions.

- Mix everything until it is combined
- Add the brownie mix to the prepared pan, and spread evenly.

- In a separate mixing bowl whisk together the cream cheese, remaining egg and the milk until smooth. Add the banana pudding mix to the cream cheese mixture and whisk again until the mixture is smooth and thick.

- Then add dollops of the banana pudding banana cream-cheese mixture on top and lightly spread, covering the brownie mix.

- You can spread or take a knife and swirl the cream-cheese mixture throughout brownie mix.
- Top with Vanilla Wafers according to your preference of placement and bake according to the directions on the brownie mix box, but add 5 minutes to baking time.

- Once done, let cool for 15 minutes before cutting into any size square pieces you desire and serve.

- Enjoy!

PRETZEL BaconCheese Burger

Prep Time : 10min
Cook Time : 15min
Servings : 1

Ingredients:

1 pack KING'S HAWAIIAN Pretzel Hamburger Buns

4 oz ground beef

1 tsp salt & pepper

your favorite seasonings

1 slice cheddar cheese

1 slice tomato

1 thin slice red onion

1/2 tbsp mayo

1/2 tbsp yellow mustard

1/2 tbsp ketchup

2 leaf lettuce pieces

2 bacon slices

2 tbsp of **INFUSED GARLIC** OR **PURPLE HAZE BUTTER**

DIRECTIONS:

To a skillet melt Infused Butter and add pretzel buns to toast. Set aside.

Wipe skillet and add bacon slices. Cook thoroughly. Drain on paper towels and set aside.

Mix ground beef with seasonings and form into a patty.

Heat grill or skillet to medium-high heat and cook hamburger patty for 4 minutes on each side.

Place bacon on hamburger patty, top with cheddar cheese and then cover grill or skillet for about 1 minute until cheese is melted.

Assemble hamburger bun with burger, condiments, red onion, tomato, lettuce, mustard and ketchup.

Notes :

Even better with fries or chips and a pickle on the side.

WE DO NOT COUNT CALORIES OVER HEA

Lazy Lasagna

Cook Time: 1:45min
Servings: 12

Ingredients:

12 lasagna noodles uncooked
4 cups mozzarella cheese shredded and divided
½ cup parmesan cheese shredded and divided
Tomato Sauce
Between 2 teaspoons and 1/3 cup of **INFUSED GARLIC** OR **PURPLE HAZE BUTTER**
½ pound lean ground beef
½ pound Italian sausage
1 onion diced
2 cloves garlic minced
36 ounces pasta sauce *see note
2 tablespoons tomato paste
1 teaspoon Italian seasoning
2 cups ricotta cheese
¼ cup fresh parsley chopped
1 egg beaten

Directions

- Preheat the oven to 350°F. In a large pot of salted water, boil lasagna noodles until al dente according to package directions. Drain, rinse under cold water, and set aside.

- In a large skillet or dutch oven, brown beef, sausage, onion, and garlic over medium-high heat until no pink remains. Drain any fat.

- Stir in the pasta sauce, tomato paste, desired amount of infused butter, Italian seasoning, ½ teaspoon of salt, and ¼ teaspoon of black pepper. Simmer uncovered over medium heat for 5 minutes or until thickened.

- In a separate bowl, combine 1 ½ cups mozzarella, ¼ cup parmesan cheese, ricotta, parsley, egg, desired amount of infused butter, and ¼ teaspoon salt.

- Spread 1 cup of the meat sauce in a 9×13 pan or casserole dish. Top it with 3 lasagna noodles. Layer with ⅓ of the ricotta cheese mixture and 1 cup of meat sauce. Repeat twice more. Finish with 3 noodles topped with remaining sauce.

- Cover with foil and bake for 45 minutes.

- Remove the foil and sprinkle with the remaining 2 ½ cups mozzarella cheese and ¼ cup parmesan cheese. Bake for an additional 15 minutes or until browned and bubbly. Broil for 2-3 minutes if desired.

- Rest for at least 15 minutes before cutting. SERVE.

PILE UP YOUR PLATE SIS!

Honey Lemon Pepper
Tenders & Fries

Ingredients :

- 6pack favorite chicken tenderloins
- 1 bag of steak cute or crinkle fries
- S&P to taste
- Favorite seasoings
- 3 tbsp Lemon pepper Seasoning
- 1/2 cup Honey
- 1/3 cup Infused Purple Haze Butter
- 2 tbsp olive oil
- 2 cups of flour
- 3 whisked eggs
- Cooking oil

Prep Time : 10 min.

Cook Time : 20 min.

Servings : 6 tenders

Directions

Wash and dry the chicken. Add to a plate and toss in olive oil. Then season chicken breast with favorite seasonings.

Prepare 2 bowls. One for flour and one for whisked eggs.

One by one, dip each chicken tender first in flour, beaten egg, and then back in flour.

Warm up cooking oil in a large nonstick skillet over medium-high heat. Cook chicken for 4 minutes on both sides or until golden brown and crispy. To ensure chicken doneness, use a kitchen thermometer to register 165 degrees Fahrenheit inserted into the thickest part of the chicken.

Set aside on a plate with a paper towel to absorb the excess oil. Add your french fries to the oil and cook for 5-6 minutes. Remove when done and drain on a paper towel lined bowl.

Melt 1/3 cup of Infused Purple Haze butter in sauce pan. Add 1/2 cup of honey and 3 table spoons of Lemon Pepper Seasoning.

Once combined, fully toss tenders in lemon pepper honey butter sauce and serve alongside french fries and your favorite dipping sauce.

**WE DO
NOT
COUNT
CALORIES
OVER
HEA**

Mixed Berry Shortcake Jars

Prep Time : 15   Cook Time : 40   Servings : 4

INGREDIENTS

1 cup All Purpose Flour

2 tsp Baking Powder

1/8 tsp Baking Soda

2 Tbsp Light Brown Sugar

1 tsp Salt

4 Tbsp (1/2 stick) store bought butter

1/3 cup Infused Purple Haze Butter

1/2 -3/4 cup Buttermilk

1 pint of Mixed Berries (about 2 cups)

2 Tbsp Granulated Sugar

1 cup of very cold Heavy Whipping Cream

2 Tbsp Granulated Sugar

DIRECTIONS

- Place the berries in a large bowl and add the two Tbsp of granulated sugar and let sit while you make the shortcakes.

- Heat oven to 450 degrees. In a large bowl, combine the 1 cup of flour, 2 tsp baking powder, 1/8 tsp baking soda, 2 Tbsp light brown sugar, and 1 tsp salt. Stir well to combine.

- Cut the 1/2 stick of store bought butter into thin slices and add to the bowl of dry ingredients. Add 1/3 cup infused butter in as well.

- Using a pastry blender or two knives, cut the butter into the flour mixture until the butter pieces are pea sized.

- Add the butter milk, starting with 1/2 cup. Use a fork to stir. If the mixture still seems dry, add more buttermilk one tablespoon at a time until the mixture forms a soft shaggy dough (it shouldn't be too wet).

DIRECTIONS

- Using a large spoon, divide the dough into four pieces and drop onto a rimmed baking sheet.

- Place the baking sheet in the freezer for about 5 to 10 minutes to allow the dough to get nice and cold.

- Remove the baking sheet from the freezer and place in the oven on a lower rack. Bake for 10 to 15 minutes, until the tops are light golden and the center springs back when lightly touched. Check after 10 minutes, then every 1-2 minutes after to avoid over baking.

- Once biscuits are done, remove from the oven to allow to cool while you make the whipped cream.

- In a stand mixer with the whisk attachment or a large bowl and a hand mixer with whisk attachment, mix the cream and 2 Tbsp of granulated sugar on medium high speed until stiff peaks form.

DIRECTIONS

- This could take a few minutes, but keep checking by stopping the mixer and turning the whisk attachment upside down. If the cream stands straight up on the end of the whisk, you're at the right place. Don't over whip or you will end up with butter!

- Make sure your jars are clean. You will use one shortcake for each jar. Cut the shortcakes into cubes about a half inch to one inch in size. Place half the cubes of each shortcake into the bottom of the jars.

- Add a spoonful of whipped cream on top of the biscuit cubes. You may need two or three spoons of whipped cream to cover the shortcake pieces.

- Next, add a few berries on top of the whipped cream.

- Repeat these steps until you reach the top of the jars. If you are careful about dividing your ingredients, you should run out at the same time you reach the top of your jars.

ENJOY!!!

JUST EAT IT!

Hips, Thighs, & DINNER ROLLS

Ingridients :

1 envelope active dried yeast

½ cup water about room temperature warm,

1 cup milk whole milk or 2% preferred

4 tablespoons melted store bought butter

1/3 cup of melted INFUSED PURPLE HAZE BUTTER

2 tablespoons sugar

4 cups all-purpose flour or more if needed

½ tablespoon salt

1 egg for egg wash

Prep: 30 mins   Cook: 20mins   Rise: 1 hr   Servings: 12 rolls

Directions:

- Whisk the yeast into the warm water in a small bowl and set aside until bubbles start to appear on the surface.

- In the meantime, whisk together the milk, all the melted butter and sugar. Add the activated yeast mixture and whisk until combined.

- Add the flour and salt to the bowl of your stand mixer fitted with the hook attachment. Add the milk mixture, then knead on medium–low speed for 5–6 minutes, or until you have a smooth ball of dough. Add an extra tablespoon of flour if your dough feels too sticky!

- Cover the bowl with a clean kitchen towel and let stand at room temperature for 1 hour, or until doubled in size. Punch down, then divide dough into 12 equal pieces; shape into balls. Place in greased 9×11 inch baking pan. Cover and let rise at room temperature until big and puffed up, about 20–30 minutes.

- Heat the oven to 375°F. Beat the egg and egg wash the top of the rolls (you will most likely not use the entire egg; don't add too much or you'll have scrambled eggs on top of your rolls). Bake for around 20 minutes or until done. Brush with additional melted infused butter right as they come out of the oven, if you like. Remove from the pan and serve warm.

STOP WORRYING ABOUT YOUR WEIGHT, JUST EAT!

AUNTIE'S INFUSED PEACH HENNESSY BUNDT

Prep Time: 25mins
Cook Time : 4 hrs
Servings   : 12

Ingredients :

1 ¾ cups store bought butter, softened, divided

2 cups firmly packed light brown sugar, divided

4 peaches, peeled and cut into 4 slices

1 (8-oz.) package cream cheese, softened

1 ½ cups granulated sugar

6 large eggs

1 ½ teaspoons vanilla extract, divided

3 cups all-purpose flour

½ teaspoon salt

¼ cup (2 oz.) Hennessy

1 cup powdered sugar

1 to 2 tablespoons milk

1/3 cup **INFUSED PURPLE HAZE BUTTER**

Directions

- Preheat oven to 325°F. Melt ¼ cup of the store bought butter and all of the infused butter in a small saucepan over medium heat. Stir in ½ cup of the brown sugar. Cook, whisking constantly, until sugar has dissolved and mixture is thoroughly combined, about 1 minute. Pour mixture evenly into a 15-cup (10 ½-inch) Bundt pan that has been heavily greased with cooking spray.

- Place peach slices in an even layer on top of brown sugar mixture.

- Beat cream cheese and remaining 1 ½ cups butter with a heavy-duty stand mixer on medium speed until creamy, about 1 minute. Gradually add granulated sugar and remaining 1 ½ cups brown sugar, beating on medium speed until light and fluffy, 3 to 5 minutes. Add eggs, 1 at a time, beating just until yolk disappears. Beat in 1 teaspoon of the vanilla.

Directions

- Sift together flour and salt; add to butter mixture alternately with Hennessy, beginning and ending with flour mixture. Spoon batter carefully over peaches in prepared pan; level with a spatula.

- Bake in preheated oven until a long wooden pick inserted in center of cake comes out clean, 1 hour and 25 minutes to 1 hour and 30 minutes. Cool in pan on a wire rack until pan is cool enough to handle but still hot, about 25 minutes. Remove cake from pan to rack, and cool completely, about 2 hours.

- Stir together powdered sugar, remaining ½ teaspoon vanilla, and 1 tablespoon of the milk in a small bowl, adding remaining 1 tablespoon milk, 1 teaspoon at a time, if needed to reach desired consistency. Drizzle over cooled cake.

WE DO
NOT
COUNT
CALORIES
OVER
HEA

"EUPHORIA"

COOK WITH THIS SPICE FOR THE BEST EUPHORIC BODY HIGH YOU CAN GET FROM INFUSED FOOD. THE BLEND OF SPICES ARE BOLD, INFUSED, AND SPRINKLED WITH MAJIC. BAKED AND BOTTLED TO KICK THE HELL OUT OF EVERY DISH! THIS SPICE IS MADE WITH MANY OF YOUR FAVORITE SPICES FROM YOUR OWN KITCHENS. I ADDED A LITTLE RAZZLE DAZZLE TO LIFT YOU UP OFF YOUR FEET WHEN EATING!

WWW.JSNACKS.COM

AUNTIE'S INFUSED BUTTERS

SEAFOOD

8OZ JAR OF INFUSED BUTTER 🧈 SLOW COOKED AND WHIPPED. GREAT FOR YOUR SHRIMP, CRABS, SEAFOOD BOILS, AND GUMBO. DID I MENTION THIS BUTTER IS INFUSED WITH HIGH GRADE FLOWER 🌼💨 PERFECT FOR ANXIETY, INSOMNIA, CHRONIC PAINS, AND MORE!

WWW.JSNACKS.COM

AUNTIE'S INFUSED BUTTERS

GARLIC HERB

8OZ JAR OF INFUSED GARLIC BUTTER 🧈 ROASTED GARLIC AND BUTTER, SLOW COOKED AND WHIPPED. GREAT FOR YOUR STEAKS, BAKED POTATOES, VEGGIES, GARLIC BREADS, GRILLED CHEESES, AND SATUEEING. DID I MENTION THIS BUTTER IS INFUSED WITH HIGH GRADE FLOWER 🌿 PERFECT FOR ANXIETY, INSOMNIA, CHRONIC PAINS, AND MORE!

WWW.JSNACKS.COM

AUNTIE'S INFUSED BUTTERS

PURPLE HAZE

8OZ JAR OF INFUSED PURPLE HAZE BUTTER 🧈 SLOW COOKED AND WHIPPED FOR HOURS. GREAT FOR YOUR EGGS 🥚 MAC N CHEESE 🧀 AND BAKED POTATO 🥔 BREADS, BISCUITS, SAUCES, DESSERTS AND MORE. DID I MENTION THIS BUTTER IS INFUSED WITH HIGH GRADE FLOWER (PURPLE HAZE STRAIN) 🌿 PERFECT FOR ANXIETY, INSOMNIA, CHRONIC PAINS, AND MORE!

WWW.JSNACKS.COM

"Blunts and Baking" is not your average cookbook – it's a bold exploration of urban culture and culinary creativity infused with the power of cannabis. Designed for those who appreciate the HIGHER things in life, this cookbook offers a tantalizing array of recipes that seamlessly blend the LOVE of CANNABIS with the craft of COOKING."

---- Auntie Bee

Blunts & Baking

Made in the USA
Columbia, SC
20 February 2025